EXERCISES FOR SENIORS OVER SIXTY

Aaron Wright

EXERCISES FOR SENIORS OVER SIXTY

3-in-1 Book with Pictures, Core Exercises, Strength Training, Balance & Stretching Workout, Quick & Simple Physical Activities Under 20 Minutes A Day.

TABLE OF CONTENTS

INTRODUCTION

WHY SHOULD YOU EXERCISE?

One of the most advantageous things you can do for yourself as an adult is engage in regular physical activities. It can help you prevent various health problems often related to old age. Also, it enables you to keep doing your daily activities without being dependent on others by helping your muscles to grow stronger.

Without regular exercise, people over the age of 50 years can experience a range of health problems, including reduced muscle mass, strength, and physical endurance, reduced coordination and balance, and reduced joint flexibility and mobility.

Adults need at least 150 minutes of moderate-intensity activity like brisk walking every week. That can be spread out over the week for like 30 minutes five times daily. Adults also need at least two days of activities that strengthen muscles. Adults aged 60 and above should add activities to improve balance, such as standing on one foot. Adults who cannot meet the physical activity guidelines should be as active as their abilities or conditions allow.

Here are some indicators of lack of exercise:

- Constipation
- Stiffen Joints
- Always Running Out of Breath
- Tiredness or Sluggishness
- Slow Metabolism
- Regular Forgetfulness
- High Blood Pressure
- Prediabetes
- Back Pain
- Regular Sickness

• Dull Skin

If you are experiencing any of those symptoms, don't lose hope because a solution is here for you. You will be surprised by how much improvement you will feel after doing the exercises covered in this book.

SO, WHAT ARE THE BENEFITS OF REGULAR EXERCISE?

As an adult, regular exercise will give you improved health and quality life. Physical activity will help reduce the risk of moderate or severe functional limitations and also the risk of premature death. When you exercise regularly, you will have improved mental health and healthy aging.

Here is a bonus: exercising will help you cut costs by reducing how much you spend on healthcare.

WHAT WILL HAPPEN IF I REFUSE TO EXERCISE REGULARLY?

A sedentary life is very risky for an adult. Refusing to regularly exercise might cause some biological downtime that will expose you to chronic illnesses like:

• Cardiovascular Disease

• Cancer

• Musculoskeletal Deterioration

• Type 2 Diabetes

• Mental Fog

Therefore, if you are yet to start exercising, it is not too late! The exercises in this book are guaranteed to strengthen every necessary area of your body system so that you can live a healthy life and remain forever young. This book consists of Balance Exercises to improve your coordination, Strength Training Exercises to make you stronger and improve your resistance, and Core Training Exercises to improve your posture, balance, and endurance.

However, do not forget to check the bonus page where you will have access to ethical and healthy practices that will help boost the effect of these exercises on you, and at the end, look like you are just thirty years old.

Are you ready to start? I can't wait to see you through to the last page.

CORE TRAINING EXERCISES

Core exercises are exercises that focus on strengthening the abdominal muscles, back muscles, and pelvic floor muscles. These muscles play a vital role in supporting the spine, maintaining good posture, and controlling movement.

In this chapter you will have access to easy core exercises that will help offer these benefits to your body while keeping you fit:

Longer Life: If you want to be free from chronic illness that might lead to death, then core exercises can help you achieve that. They help to reduce the risk of chronic diseases such as heart disease, stroke, and diabetes.

Anti-Aging: Core exercises can help slow the aging process by keeping the muscles strong and flexible. This can lead to improved posture, reduced aches and pains, and a more youthful appearance.

Reduced Risk ff Injury: Having a strong core will save your spine and other joints from injury. This is important for people of all ages, but it is especially important for people who are active or who have a history of injuries.

Improved Posture: Strong core muscles help to keep the spine in alignment, which can lead to improved posture. This can make you look and feel taller and more confident.

Reduced Stress: Core exercises can help to reduce stress by releasing endorphins, which have mood-boosting effects.

The exercises in this chapter—which feature those you can do on seats, stand, mat, and some with dumbbells—are a great way to improve your overall health and well-being. They can help you to live longer, healthier, and more active lives.

As you flip this page to the other, ensure to start with the first core exercise and continue.

SEATED EXERCISES

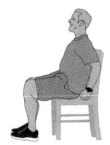

1. **KNEE LIFTS**

    Knee Lifts imitate the motion of getting out of a car, and they are beneficial for improving stability and strength in the lower abs and upper legs, which is essential for climbing stairs.

    INSTRUCTIONS:

    1. Sit up straight in a chair and hold the sides for support if needed. Take a deep breath.

    2. Exhale and engage your abdominal muscles as you lift your right leg with your knee bent at a 90-degree angle. Inhale as you lower the leg.

    3. Repeat the same motion on the other side. Completing both sides counts as one repetition (rep).

    4. Start with 10 reps and gradually increase to 20 reps as you progress.

    MODIFICATION: For an added challenge, you can use ankle weights to increase resistance.

2. **DIAGONAL CRUNCH**

The Diagonal Crunch is a low-impact exercise that helps tone the muscles responsible for the "six-pack" appearance without straining your neck, which can sometimes happen with regular crunches. The seated position also aids in improving balance.

INSTRUCTIONS:

1. Sit down with both feet on the floor and your hands on your head. Take a deep breath.

2. Exhale and tighten your abdominal muscles. Lift your right leg while simultaneously crunching your left elbow downward towards your right knee.

3. Inhale as you lower your leg and return to the upright position.

4. Repeat the same motion on the other side. Completing both sides counts as one repetition (rep).

5. Aim for 10 reps initially and gradually increase to 20 reps over time.

MODIFICATION: For more intensity, you can add ankle weights to increase resistance.

3.   **SEATED SIDE BEND:**

The Seated Side Bend targets the muscles along the spine, which are involved in various daily activities such as bending to pick up objects or tying shoes. Strengthening these muscles is essential for maintaining proper posture and preventing back pain.

INSTRUCTIONS:

1. Sit in a chair with your hands hanging down over the sides. Take a deep breath.

2. Exhale and engage your core. Bend to the right, reaching your right hand towards the floor.

3. Inhale as you return to the upright position. This completes one repetition (rep).

4. Repeat the movement 8 to 10 times and then switch to the other side.

MODIFICATION: For added resistance, you can hold a dumbbell.

4. **SEATED TWIST:**

The Seated Twist targets the muscles involved in checking blind spots while driving, which is essential for road safety. This exercise helps improve your ability to change direction quickly and also works on reducing love handles.

INSTRUCTIONS:

1. Sit upright with your hands clasped and arms in front of your chest. Take a deep breath.

2. Exhale as you twist to one side, engaging your core muscles tightly around your spine, like a corset.

3. Inhale as you return to the center, then exhale and twist to the other side. Completing both sides counts as one repetition (rep).

4. Aim for three sets of 8 to 10 reps.

MODIFICATION: For added resistance, you can hold a dumbbell or a medicine ball.

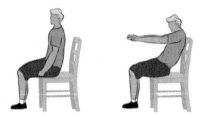

5. **SLOW RECLINE:**

The Slow Recline exercise is effective for strengthening the muscles required for sitting up comfortably in bed, getting up from a soft sofa, or rising from the floor after a workout.

INSTRUCTIONS:

1. Sit at the edge of the chair with your arms extended in front of you, palms up. Take a deep breath.

2. Exhale as you slowly recline towards the back of the chair, rounding your spine into a concave "C" shape. Don't fully relax in the chair; keep some tension in your muscles.

3. Inhale as you return to an upright position. This completes one repetition (rep).

4. Aim for 10 reps.

MODIFICATION: To make it less challenging, you can place your hands on your hips or hold the edges of the chair.

6.   **ROPE PULLS:**

Rope Pulls are beneficial for increasing your range of motion and strengthening the lats, which are crucial for everyday activities like pulling, lifting, and reaching.

INSTRUCTIONS:

1. Begin in a seated position. Inhale and reach your right arm across your body, bringing your torso forward to a 45-degree angle.

2. Make a fist as if you're grabbing an imaginary rope. Exhale as you pull your elbow backward, bringing your fist in line with your armpit and returning your torso to an upright position.

3. This completes one repetition (rep). Aim for 8 to 10 reps on each side.

MODIFICATION: For more challenge, increase the range of motion by twisting to look over your shoulder on the pull and touching your elbow to the chair behind you.

7. **AB CIRCLES:**

Ab Circles promote proper posture and counteract the negative effects of prolonged sitting, preventing muscle deterioration and back pain caused by prolonged desk work.

INSTRUCTIONS:

1. Sit forward on the edge of your chair with arms outstretched to the sides. Take a deep breath.

2. Exhale as you push your chest forward and around to one side, making a complete circle.

3. Maintain steady breathing as you complete 8 to 10 full circles. Repeat the same on the other side.

MODIFICATION: Hold weights in your outstretched hands or cross your arms on your chest for more challenge.

8. **STRAIGHT LEG CRUNCH:**

The Straight Leg Crunch not only works the core but also strengthens the hip flexors, which are crucial for activities like bending, kicking, and walking. Weak hip flexors can lead to painful injuries if sudden movements cause them to tear.

INSTRUCTIONS:

1. Start in a seated position with your right leg extended straight in front of you and arms outstretched to the sides. Take a deep breath.

2. Exhale as you crunch forward, lifting your leg off the floor and reaching your arms towards your foot.

3. Inhale as you return to the starting position. Completing both sides counts as one repetition (rep).

4. Aim for 8 to 10 reps and then switch to the other side.

MODIFICATION: To decrease intensity, keep both feet on the ground, or for added challenge, use ankle weights.

9.   **METRONOME:**

Metronome exercise involves side-to-side movements that lengthen and strengthen the obliques, important for trunk stabilization. A strong, stable trunk is essential for lifting heavy objects and preventing hyperextension of the back.

INSTRUCTIONS:

1. Sit forward on the edge of your chair with arms extended overhead and palms touching. Take a deep breath.

2. In a fluid, controlled motion, move your torso from side to side, as if swinging like a metronome to about 10 o'clock and 2 o'clock positions if you were looking at a clock face.

3. Breathe steadily as you perform 10 to 12 cycles of the movement. Focus on steady breathing rather than specific inhalation and exhalation timings.

MODIFICATION: For more core challenges, lift your hip off the chair for two seconds as you lean to each side. Repeat on the other side.

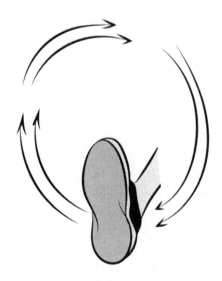

10.   ANKLE CIRCLES:

Ankle Circles exercise is a dynamic stretch that helps to reduce stress, tension, and fatigue in your ankle.

INSTRUCTIONS:

1. Sit on a chair maintaining a straight back posture

2. Sit firmly on the chair for stability by holding it with your two hands

3. Then rotate your right foot in circles like you are tracing an imaginary circle

4. Repeat the same procedure on each foot for 10-20 rotations.

STANDING EXERCISES

11. **STANDING CRUNCH:**

Standing crunches effectively engage the deep core muscles, providing stability throughout your midsection and reducing the risk of injury. Unlike traditional crunches, standing crunches target the inner core muscles more effectively.

INSTRUCTIONS:

1. Stand with your feet hip-width apart and place your hands behind your head. Take a deep breath.

2. Exhale as you raise your right knee while crunching your left elbow across your body towards your knee. Pull your core inward during the movement.

3. Inhale as you return to the starting position. Repeat the same on the other side. Completing both sides counts as one repetition (rep).

4. Aim to complete a set of 20 reps.

MODIFICATION: To decrease intensity, perform the crunch without lifting your knee. For added intensity, increase the number of reps or try using ankle weights.

12. **SIDE BENDS:**

Side Bends strengthen and increase the flexibility of your lower back, helping to prevent back injuries. Additionally, they build the muscles supporting the spine, promote good posture, and shape the waist.

INSTRUCTIONS:

1. Stand with your feet hip-width apart, arms at your sides, and gently bend your knees. Take a deep breath.

2. Exhale as you contract your side abdominal wall and bend to the right side, reaching your right fingertips towards the floor.

3. Inhale as you return to the starting position. This completes one repetition (rep). Aim for 10 to 15 reps on both sides.

MODIFICATION: To increase the challenge, hold a dumbbell in each hand or perform the exercise with your hands clasped overhead, similar to the motion of the Metronome exercise.

13. **SIDE CRUNCH WITH LEG LIFT:**

The Side Crunch with Leg Lift enhances your balance for daily activities, making it easier to bend over to pick up items or put on your shoes without the need to sit down. This exercise targets the obliques and erector spinae muscles, which play a vital role in stabilizing the body during waist-bending movements.

INSTRUCTIONS:

1. Stand with your feet hip-width apart and place your hands behind your head. Take a deep breath.

2. Exhale as you open your right hip and lift your right knee to the side of your body. Simultaneously, crunch your right elbow down to meet your knee.

3. Inhale as you return to the starting position. Completing both sides counts as one repetition (rep).

4. Aim for 8 reps on each side.

MODIFICATION: To decrease intensity, perform the crunch with both feet on the floor. For added intensity, increase the number of reps or use ankle weights.

14. **PELVIC TILT:**

The Pelvic Tilt targets your core and hip muscles simultaneously. These muscles are crucial for standing comfortably without pain and performing movements like bending over to touch your toes or deadlift exercises that involve picking objects off the floor.

INSTRUCTIONS:

1. Stand up straight with your hands on your hips, feet shoulder-width apart, and knees slightly bent. Take a deep breath.

2. Exhale as you contract your abdominal muscles and tilt your pelvis forward, creating a concave shape with your chest. Your shoulders may move forward slightly.

3. Inhale as you return to the neutral position. This completes one repetition (rep).

4. Aim for 15 to 20 reps.

MODIFICATION: If you're a beginner, try doing this exercise with your back against a wall to feel the difference between the "neutral" and "engaged" positions.

15. **TORSO TWISTS:**

Torso Twists are beneficial for enhancing rotational ability, which is essential for various movements in daily life, including activities like golf swings. They also strengthen the muscles that protect the spine, reducing the risk of back injuries.

INSTRUCTIONS:

1. Stand with your feet hip-width apart, arms extended in front of you at shoulder level with clasped hands. Take a deep breath.

2. Engage your core and exhale as you twist to one side, looking in the direction of your twist.

3. Inhale as you return to the center and then exhale as you twist to the opposite side. This completes one repetition (rep).

4. Aim for 10 to 15 reps.

MODIFICATION: For an added challenge, hold a kettlebell, medicine ball, or dumbbell while performing the exercise.

16. **WOOD CHOP:**

The Wood Chop exercise is beneficial for sports involving racket movements like tennis, racquetball, or pickleball. It improves the range of motion and flexibility of the spine while engaging the transverse abdominis, obliques, and latissimus dorsi muscles.

INSTRUCTIONS:

1. Stand with your feet slightly wider than hip-width apart, clasping your hands in front of you with straight arms.

2. Inhale as you reach your arms diagonally up to the right side, pivoting your hips towards the right and shifting your weight to your right foot.

3. Exhale as you bring your arms downward and diagonally across your body in a chopping motion. Bend at the waist and twist down towards your left, shifting your weight to your left foot. End with your hands just outside your left shin.

4. This completes one repetition (rep). Aim for 10 to 12 reps on the right side and then repeat on the left side.

MODIFICATION: To increase the challenge, hold a kettlebell, medicine ball, or dumbbell during the exercise.

17. **TRIANGLE:**

Triangle, also known as Trikonasana in yoga, is an excellent core strengthener that improves spine flexibility, releases tension in the back, opens the hips, and stretches the hamstrings.

INSTRUCTIONS:

1. Begin in a standing position with feet wider than hip-width apart.

2. Turn your right toes outward so they point to the right. Inhale as you raise your arms to shoulder level.

3. Engage your core by pulling your belly button towards your spine. Exhale as you bend sideways at the waist, lowering your right hand down towards your outer right shin.

4. Hold the pose for three to four breath cycles, then return to a standing position. Repeat on the other side. One pose on each side is enough.

MODIFICATION: To make it easier, bring your hand to your thigh instead of your shin. For an extra challenge, try reaching your hand all the way to the floor.

18. **DIAGONAL SIT BACK:**

The Diagonal Sit Back exercise simulates the motion of reaching up for an object on a high shelf, improving balance and strengthening the core.

INSTRUCTIONS:

1. Stand angled slightly toward the right, with your left and right feet pointing in the same direction as your shoulders.

2. Inhale while reaching both arms up toward the right corner, shifting your weight to your front foot.

3. Exhale and engage your core as you bend forward at the waist, bringing your arms to your sides and sitting back into your left hip. Shift your weight to your back foot with your back knee slightly bent.

4. Return to the upright position. This completes one repetition (rep). Aim for 10 to 12 reps, then repeat on the other side.

MODIFICATION: To test your core strength and balance further, raise your back foot off the ground behind you and reach higher as you lean forward to the corner before continuing back into the crunch position.

19.   **LUNGING PULL-DOWN:**

The Lunging Pull-Down exercise targets the core muscles involved in overhead movements like reaching for objects on high shelves or closing sash windows. It also works on toning the love handles.

INSTRUCTIONS:

1. Stand with your feet wider than hip-width apart, toes slightly turned outward.

2. Inhale as you lunge to the right, reaching your left arm overhead in the direction of your lunge and the right arm by your ear.

3. Exhale as you tighten your core and move back through the center, lunging on the left side. Bend at the waist and bring your left elbow down towards your hip, continuing down to reach your left hand to your left ankle.

4. This completes one repetition (rep). Aim for 10 to 12 reps and then perform the exercise on the other side.

MODIFICATION: To make it easier, bring your arm to your knee or thigh instead of your ankle during the downward motion.

20. **CROSS PULL-DOWN:**

The cross-pull-down exercise not only targets the core muscles but also enhances the shoulder and arm range of motion. These movements play a significant role in preventing falls, as instinctively using your arms to steady yourself during a balance loss is a natural response.

INSTRUCTIONS:

1. Stand with your feet wider than hip-width apart, toes slightly turned outward.

2. Inhale as you lunge to the right, reaching your right arm up overhead in the direction of your lunge.

3. Exhale and engage your core as you move back through center, lunging on the left side. Bend at the waist and bring your right arm down and across your body toward your left ankle.

4. This completes one repetition (rep). Aim for 10 to 12 reps, then repeat the exercise on the other side.

MODIFICATION: To make it easier, bring your arm to your knee or thigh instead of your ankle during the downward motion

MAT EXERCISES

21. **KNEELING PLANK:**

The Kneeling Plank is an isometric exercise that strengthens the core muscles, including the abs, arms, shoulders, and lower back. Holding this position challenges your core by resisting gravity without any movement.

INSTRUCTIONS:

1. Start on all fours with your hands directly under your shoulders. Place your elbows where your palms are, so your forearms rest on the mat.

2. Gradually walk your knees backward to extend your torso into a straight line, with your belly suspended above the mat.

3. Keep your spine straight, engage your abdominal muscles, and hold the position while breathing in and out. Aim to hold the pose for 30 seconds.

MODIFICATION: Once you can hold the kneeling plank for 30 seconds with proper form, progress to a traditional plank by raising your knees off the ground.

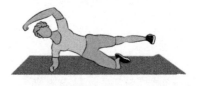

22. **MODIFIED SIDE PLANK:**

The Modified Side Plank is an isometric exercise that works the obliques, helping to shape and strengthen your waist and entire core.

INSTRUCTIONS:

1. Sit on the mat with your weight on your right hip and legs bent to your left side. Place your right elbow directly beneath your right shoulder, supporting your upper body with your forearm on the mat.

2. Keep your bottom knee bent and straighten your top leg. Lift your right hip off the mat, aligning your torso with your hip. Reach your left arm overhead.

3. Engage your core and hold the pose, breathing in and out, while avoiding dropping your right hip. Work up to holding the position for 30 seconds, then repeat on the other side.

MODIFICATION: Progress to a traditional side plank by straightening your bottom leg instead of keeping it bent.

23. **SINGLE LEG LIFTS:**

Single-leg lifts engage your core to stabilize your body as you lift one leg. This exercise helps strengthen your midsection for activities such as carrying groceries.

INSTRUCTIONS:

1. Lie on your back with your right leg straight, and your left leg bent, left foot flat on the ground. Keep your arms relaxed at your sides. Inhale.

2. Exhale and engage your core as you lift your right leg to align with your left knee. Hold for 2 seconds, then lower your right leg with control while inhaling. This completes one repetition (rep).

3. Aim for 10 to 12 reps, then repeat on the opposite side.

MODIFICATION: For an added challenge, cross your arms on your chest while maintaining space between your chin and chest.

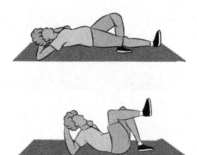

24.   **ONE-LEGGED CRUNCH:**

The One-Legged Crunch effectively engages the entire core by incorporating leg movement, making it more effective than traditional crunches.

INSTRUCTIONS:

1. Lie on your back with your right leg straight, and your left leg bent, left foot flat on the ground. Place your hands behind your head. Inhale.

2. As you exhale, bend your right knee and lift your head off the mat, crunching toward the center. Keep space between your chin and chest, by imagining holding an orange in that space.

3. Inhale as you lower your right leg back to the floor. This completes one rep. Aim for 10 to 12 reps, then switch to the other side.

MODIFICATION: For increased difficulty, stretch your arms overhead by your ears and maintain the position as you crunch up, avoiding bringing the arms forward to use momentum.

25. **CAT COW:**

Cat Cow is a gentle yet effective exercise for the lower back and sciatica pain relief. It strengthens and stretches various muscles, including the neck, shoulders, spine, and hips while providing a pleasant massage to the internal organs.

INSTRUCTIONS:

1. Start on all fours with your palms under your shoulders, maintain knees under your hips, and maintain a straight spine while looking down at the mat.

2. Inhale as you drop your belly towards the mat, lifting your chin to gaze upward. Draw your shoulders away from your ears and lengthen your belly. This is the "cow" position.

3. Exhale as you engage your core, rounding your back towards the ceiling. Release your neck and let your head drop forward, without forcing your chin to your chest. This is the "cat" position.

4. Move back and forth slowly between cow and cat, breathing mindfully for five to ten repetitions.

MODIFICATION: If your knees or wrists feel uncomfortable, use extra cushioning or support by resting your forearms on the mat instead of your palms.

26. **ALTERNATING SUPERHERO:**

The Alternating Superhero exercise targets the muscles that wrap around your entire midsection, including the sides and back, which are crucial for maintaining proper posture and preventing a hunched spine as you age.

INSTRUCTIONS:

1. Lie face down on the mat with your arms stretched overhead. Inhale.

2. Exhale and raise your right arm and left leg a few inches off the ground, engaging your core to stabilize your body. Hold for 3 seconds, then release as you inhale.

3. Switch to the other side, raising your left arm and right leg off the ground, holding for 3 seconds. This completes one repetition (rep). Aim for a set of 10 to 15 reps.

MODIFICATION: Increase the tempo to perform a "swimming" motion with your arms and legs instead of holding at the top.

27. **BIRD DOG:**

Bird Dog is an effective exercise that targets muscles involved in spine extension, flexion, and rotation. It is beneficial for safe back movement and can be particularly helpful for individuals recovering from back injuries as it avoids putting pressure on the lower back.

INSTRUCTIONS:

1. Start on all fours with your palms under your shoulders and your knees directly under your hips. Gaze down toward the mat.

2. Inhale and extend your right arm straight forward and your left leg straight behind you, creating a straight line from your right fingertips to your left toes.

3. Exhale and engage your core, rounding your back, and crunching your arm and leg together toward the middle. This is one rep. Do 10 to 12 reps, then repeat on the other side.

MODIFICATION: To improve balance, lift your arm and leg a few inches off the mat first and hold for 2 to 3 seconds before adding the crunch.

28. **SIDE SWEEPS:**

Side Sweeps target the muscles that wrap around the midsection, acting like a natural girdle, supporting posture, and enabling free movement.

INSTRUCTIONS:

1. Begin in a seated position on the mat with a straight spine, legs bent in front of you, and feet flat on the mat. Reach your hands forward, keeping your arms about shoulder-width apart. Inhale.

2. Exhale and rotate your torso to the right, sweeping your right arm out and around to touch the mat behind you.

3. Inhale, engage your core, and return to the center. Repeat the sweep on the left side. This is one rep. Aim for 10 to 15 reps.

MODIFICATION: Reduce intensity by removing the arm sweep and performing the twist with your hands clasped in front of you or placed to the side of each hip on the mat.

29. **LEVER CRUNCH:**

The Lever Crunch strengthens the muscles that help you get up from a lying position, an essential skill for daily activities.

INSTRUCTIONS:

1. Lie flat on your back, legs bent in front of you, feet flat on the mat. Extend your right arm straight overhead, and keep your left arm down by your side. Inhale.

2. Exhale, contract your core, and raise your right shoulder off the mat, sweeping your right arm up and over toward your left hip like a lever.

3. Inhale and return to the starting position. This is one rep. Do 10 to 12 reps on each side.

MODIFICATION: Stay up with your arm across your body and reach out towards the corner for eight pulses after each rep.

30.   **BRIDGE:**

The Bridge is beneficial for loosening tight muscles due to prolonged sitting, improving hip range of motion, and relieving hip and lower back pain.

INSTRUCTIONS:

1. Lie flat on your back with your legs bent, and let your feet be flat on the mat about hip-width apart. Rest your arms at your sides and inhale.

2. Press your heels into the mat, engage your core and glutes, and lift your pelvis towards the ceiling as you exhale. Aim to form a straight line from your shoulders to your knees.

3. Hold the position for 3 to 5 seconds, then inhale and release back to the starting position. Repeat five to ten times.

MODIFICATION: For an added challenge, once you can comfortably hold the bridge with proper form, try lifting one leg off the mat and straightening it in front of you.

EXERCISES WITH WEIGHTS

31. **DUMBBELL SIDE BEND:**

The Dumbbell Side Bend is an exercise that strengthens and improves flexibility in the lower back and the side abdominal wall. It supports the spine, enhances bending and twisting movements, and can help create definition in the waist.

INSTRUCTIONS:

1. Stand with your feet slightly wider than hip-width apart, holding a dumbbell with both hands, raised straight overhead. Inhale.

2. Exhale and engage your abs by pulling them towards your spine. Slowly bend to the right, imagining lengthening your spine during the movement.

3. Inhale as you return to an upright position, then repeat the bend towards the left side. This completes one repetition (rep). Aim for 10 to 15 reps.

MODIFICATION: If you need less intensity, practice the move with your hands on your hips before adding the dumbbell.

32. **TWISTING LUNGE:**

The Twisting Lunge is an excellent exercise that targets multiple muscle groups simultaneously, promoting strength and coordination between different parts of the body.

INSTRUCTIONS:

1. Stand with your weights at waist level, arms bent at a 90-degree angle, palms facing up. Inhale.

2. Exhale and step forward into a lunge with your right leg while simultaneously twisting your torso to the right. Let your gaze follow the direction of the twist.

3. Inhale as you return to the starting position. This is one rep. Aim for 8 to 10 reps on each side.

MODIFICATION: For less intensity, try breaking the move into two parts, first the lunge, and then the twist, instead of one steady movement.

33. **SQUAT WITH TWIST:**

Incorporating squats into exercises engages large muscle groups and can improve balance, mobility, and the ability to bend and lift during daily activities.

INSTRUCTIONS:

1. Stand with your feet slightly wider than hip-width apart, hands holding weights resting on your shoulders. Inhale.

2. Exhale as you send your hips backward and bend your knees, lowering into a squat position while keeping your chest upright.

3. Inhale and press your weight into your heels to rise back to a standing position, twisting your torso to the right.

4. Repeat the move, this time twisting to the left at the top. This is one rep. Aim for 20 repetitions.

MODIFICATION: You don't need to squat super low for this exercise to be effective. For less intensity, don't sink as far into your squat, or perform the move without weights.

34. **REACH BACKS:**

The Reach Backs exercise targets the muscles responsible for pulling your belly in, defining the waistline.

INSTRUCTIONS:

1. Stand with a dumbbell in each hand. Lift your chest, push your shoulders back and down, and allow your arms to hang slightly behind your thighs. Inhale.

2. Exhale and bend to the right, then to the left, reaching behind your knee on either side. This is one rep.

3. Continue breathing as you bend from side to side. Aim for 20 total reps.

MODIFICATION: Increase the dumbbell weight or perform additional reps several times in a row on either side and then reverse.

35. **WEIGHTED PULL-DOWNS:**

Weighted Pull-Downs strengthen muscles and maintain the range of motion needed for various activities like putting away groceries, hanging decorations, and performing yard work.

INSTRUCTIONS:

1. Stand upright, holding a dumbbell in each hand at chest level with arms bent.

2. Inhale and reach up and to the right, shifting your weight onto your right foot.

3. Exhale, engage your core, and bring the weight down through the center and across your body, squatting as you shift your weight to your left leg, bringing the weight to the outside of your left shin.

4. This is one rep. Perform 8 to 10 reps, then repeat on the other side.

MODIFICATION: Increase the dumbbell weight or perform additional reps for more intensity.

36. **PUNCHING KICKS:**

Punching Kicks improve balance, coordination, and muscle memory, benefiting daily movement and posture. Light weights are commonly used for this exercise.

INSTRUCTIONS:

1. Stand with a dumbbell in each hand, biceps curled. Inhale.

2. Exhale and extend your right arm forward in a punching motion while simultaneously kicking your left leg forward.

3. Return to the center and switch to a punch and kick on the other side. This is one rep. Aim to complete 20 reps.

MODIFICATION: Increase the weight or add reps for more intensity.

37. **CRUNCHING TWISTS:**

The Crunching Twists exercise combines a squat with a twist, providing strength and toning to the targeted muscles. It enhances your ability to perform tasks closer to the ground and improves core stability, making it useful for activities like gardening, bending to pick things up, or getting out of bed.

INSTRUCTIONS:

1. Face to your right with your weight on your right foot, knees slightly bent. Hold a dumbbell in each hand, with biceps curled. Inhale.

2. Exhale and engage your core as you move into a squat position in the center, bending at the waist to bring your upper body into a crunch.

3. Inhale and pivot to the left, lifting your torso to assume a standing position on the opposite side. This is one rep. Aim for 10 to 12 back-and-forth reps.

MODIFICATION: For more intensity, add an upward punch as you raise your torso to either side.

38.   ANGLED SIDE CRUNCH:

The Angled Side Crunch is an effective exercise for building core stability and avoiding side-to-side wobbling. It strengthens the muscles needed for rolling sideways and lifting yourself out of bed while reducing the risk of neck injury compared to traditional crunches.

INSTRUCTIONS:

1. Sit on the mat with your legs bent in front of you and your feet on the mat. Hold one dumbbell in both hands and raise it straight overhead, sitting up tall. Inhale.

2. Exhale as you lean backward and twist your torso to the right, bringing the weight down towards your right hip.

3. Inhale and return to the starting position. Repeat the crunch on the other side. This is one rep. Aim for 15 to 20 repetitions.

MODIFICATION: Extend your reach from the hip to the floor behind you for a longer range of motion.

39. **WEIGHTED CRUNCH:**

The Weighted Crunch is a low-impact exercise that helps build core strength effectively.

INSTRUCTIONS:

1. Lie on your back with your legs bent in front of you and your feet on the mat. Cross your arms in an X over your chest, holding a dumbbell in each hand. Inhale.

2. Exhale and engage your core to lift your chin toward the ceiling, bringing your shoulders off the mat.

3. Inhale as you lower your shoulders back down. This is one crunch. Aim for 15 to 20 crunches.

MODIFICATION: For more intensity, hold the crunch at the top for 1 to 2 seconds or add additional weight.

40. **PUNCHING CRUNCH:**

The Punching Crunch is an exercise that targets the muscles of the chest while also firming the core.

INSTRUCTIONS:

1. Lie on your back your with legs bent in front of you and feet on the mat. Bend your arms and bring the dumbbells to rest just above your armpits. Inhale.

2. Exhale and engage your core to lift your shoulders off the mat, twisting your torso toward the right. Extend your left arm upward in a punching motion.

3. Inhale as you lower your back to the mat and return to the starting position. Repeat on the opposite side. This is one crunch. Aim for 15 to 20 crunches.

MODIFICATION: For more intensity, hold the punch at the top for 1 to 2 seconds or add additional weight.

BALANCE EXERCISES

This section consists of standing, sitting, walking, and lying down balance exercises that are guaranteed to help you improve your ability to maintain balance and coordination. These simple exercises were specifically picked for older adults like you to prevent you from falling and also offer some more benefits like:

Anti-Aging

These balance exercises can help to slow down the aging process by improving your overall health and fitness. When you have a good balance, you are less likely to fall and avoid injuries and other health problems. Balance exercises can also help to improve your cardiovascular health, strength, and flexibility.

Long Life

Studies have shown that people who regularly perform balance exercises are more likely to live longer, healthier lives. This is likely because balance exercises help to reduce the risk of falls and other injuries, which are major causes of death and disability in older adults.

Improved Memory

Balance exercises can also help to improve your memory. This is because these exercises require you to use multiple cognitive functions, such as attention, coordination, and problem-solving. When you regularly perform balance exercises, you are training your brain to work more efficiently.

Improved Balance and Coordination

Of course, one of the main reasons why these exercises are included is that they can help to improve your balance and coordination. This can make it easier to perform everyday activities, such as walking, getting up from a chair, and climbing stairs. Improved balance and coordination can also help to reduce your risk of falls.

Aside from those, balance exercises can help you to reduce stress and anxiety, have quality sleep, boost your mood, improve your athletic performance, and diminish pain.

If you are new to this, it is important to start slowly and gradually increase the difficulty of the exercises as you get stronger. Here are a few simple balance exercises that you can try:

If you have any concerns about starting balance exercises, be sure to talk to your doctor first.

If you are not already doing these exercises, be sure to start today!

STANDING BALANCE EXERCISES

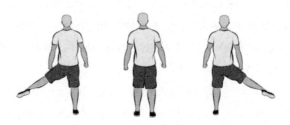

41. **ROCK THE BOAT**

Rock the Boat is a variation of weight shifting, offering similar benefits like improved balance and reduced stress and tension. This exercise enhances flexibility and mobility, allowing for better performance of daily activities. It can be done without any equipment, though external support can be used if necessary.

INSTRUCTIONS:

1. Stand with feet positioned hip-width apart.

2. Lift your left leg sideways and maintain the position for 2 seconds.

3. Return to the starting position.

4. Now, lift your right leg laterally and hold for 2 seconds.

5. Repeat the above steps for each leg, aiming for up to 10 repetitions per leg.

42. FLAMINGO STAND

Inspired by the balancing abilities of flamingos, the flamingo stand exercise strengthens the trunk, leg, and pelvic muscles, helping control dizziness and reducing vertigo symptoms.

INSTRUCTIONS:

1. Stand straight with feet hip-width apart, with a chair in front for support if needed.

2. Lift your left foot off the ground and bring it back.

3. Hold the position for 20 seconds, using your fingertips on the chair for support if necessary.

4. Return to the starting position and perform the exercise with your right leg.

5. Repeat the exercise 3 times per leg.

43.   BACK LEG RAISES

Back leg raises strengthen the back, glutes, and legs, improving posture and abdominal muscle firmness.

INSTRUCTIONS:

1. Place your hands on a walker, chair, or wall for support.

2. Shift your weight to the right side of your body.

3. Lift your left leg as high as possible backward.

4. Hold your leg in the air for five seconds, then lower it while keeping your hands on the support.

5. Repeat the steps 10 more times on the same leg.

6. Repeat all the steps on the other leg.

44.   SIDE LEG RAISES

Side leg raises are similar to back leg raises, focusing on building thigh muscles. While you can do this exercise lying down, standing provides better results. Have a counter, chair, or walker nearby for support.

INSTRUCTIONS:

1. Stand behind the support object.
2. Keep feet hip-width apart.
3. Lift your right leg to the side.
4. Maintain a straight posture and face forward.
5. Repeat the leg raise 15 times on each side.

Variation: For a different leg exercise, try moving your legs forward and backward. This exercise strengthens leg, ankle, and foot muscles and joints.

45. **MINI LUNGES**

Mini lunges strengthen legs, reducing fall risks, and improving balance control.

INSTRUCTIONS:

1. Stand with feet shoulder-width apart, holding onto something for balance if required.

2. Step your left leg directly behind you, keeping it straight.

3. Slightly bend your right knee, ensuring it aligns with your toes.

4. Hold the position for 15 seconds.

5. Stand back up straight and repeat with your other leg.

6. Do 3 repetitions for each leg.

46. **2-WAY HIP KICK**

The 2-way hip kick exercise strengthens hips, improving stability while walking and climbing stairs.

INSTRUCTIONS:

1. Stand with feet hip-width apart, using a counter or chair for support if necessary.

2. Extend your left leg fully in front of you, then bring it back to the starting position.

3. Extend the same leg to your side, then return it to the starting position.

4. Repeat these steps with the opposite leg.

5. Do this exercise 10 times on each leg.

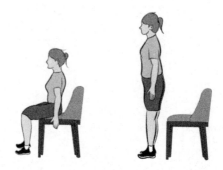

47.   **SIT TO STAND**

Sit-to-stand exercises involve moving from a sitting to a standing position, improving mobility, balance, and posture.

INSTRUCTIONS:

1. Stand in front of a chair, bend your legs, and sit down.

2. Pause briefly, then stand back up.

3. Focus on using core and leg muscles to rise and sit.

4. Repeat this process 10 times.

48.   2-POINT STANCE

The 2-point stance exercise is useful for improving flexibility, range of motion, lower body, and back muscle strength, enhancing stability, and preventing falls.

INSTRUCTIONS:

1. Stand with feet flat and shoulder-width apart.

2. Slightly bend forward, placing your hands on your knees.

3. Keep your head up, looking into the distance.

4. Hold the stance for 15 to 30 seconds.

5. Repeat 5 times or as needed.

49. **SKATER SWITCH EXERCISE**

The skater switch exercise builds muscle and bone strength, particularly in the hips, legs, and glutes. It enhances balance, coordination, and cardiovascular health, making it suitable for beginners due to its simplicity and equipment-free nature.

INSTRUCTIONS:

1. Stand straight, looking ahead.

2. Slightly bend your left knee and bring your right leg back behind the left leg.

3. Bring your arms to the left side, then switch them to the right side as you bring your right leg back to the starting position.

4. Switch legs and repeat the movement.

5. Perform this process 10 times, simulating a skating motion.

50. **DYNAMIC BALANCE**

Dynamic balance is a highly effective exercise for practicing balance in realistic situations. Daily practice can yield remarkable results. Use a chair for support.

INSTRUCTIONS:

1. Stand with feet hip-width apart, resting your hand on the back of the chair.

2. Slowly raise your left knee in front of you.

3. Find your balance and gradually lift your hand off the chair, using only your fingertips if needed.

4. Slowly bring your leg behind you, slightly bending your knee.

5. Continue the movement, bringing your leg forward and back.

6. Repeat this exercise 10 times per leg.

SITTING BALANCE EXERCISES

51. **SEATED HIP MARCHES**

Seated hip marches improve hip flexibility and mobility, and strengthen thighs and hips.

INSTRUCTIONS:

1. Sit on a chair with your back straight and feet flat on the ground, about a foot apart.

2. Hold the edge of the seat with both hands, maintaining a tall posture.

3. Lift your right leg as high as possible, keeping the knee bent.

4. Lower your right foot back to the ground, returning to the starting position.

5. Repeat with your left leg. Perform 10 repetitions on each leg.

52.   ELBOW TO OPPOSITE KNEE

This exercise enhances coordination, strengthens the neuromuscular system, and improves overall balance, reducing the risk of falls.

INSTRUCTIONS:

1. Sit with a straight back and feet flat on the ground.

2. Place your right hand behind your head, forming a sharp angle with your arm.

3. Raise your left knee and rotate your right elbow to touch your left knee.

4. Repeat the exercise 10 times.

5. Repeat with the left elbow and right knee.

53.   BAND PULL-APART

Band pull-apart strengthens arm muscles, improves posture, and enhances coordination.

INSTRUCTIONS:

1. Sit on a chair with a mini resistance band in front of you, arms outstretched, and elbows slightly bent.

2. Pull your arms to each side at shoulder height, stretching the band.

3. Repeat 10 times.

54. **MODIFIED LEG LIFTS**

Modified leg lifts strengthen the core, enhancing stability for everyday tasks.

INSTRUCTIONS:

1. Sit with knees and ankles touching each other.

2. Keep head, shoulder, and spine aligned.

3. Hold the bottom of the chair.

4. Straighten your legs out in front, lifting your feet as high as possible.

5. Hold for 5 seconds and slowly lower.

6. Repeat 10 to 12 times.

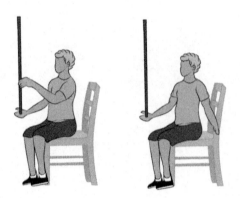

55. **BALANCING WAND**

Balancing wand exercise improves balance and coordination.

INSTRUCTIONS:

1. Hold a cane or stick while seated.

2. Balance it on your palm.

3. Switch hands every 30 to 60 seconds.

4. Repeat 3 times per arm.

56. **SEATED JUMPING JACKS**

Seated jumping jacks improve balance, coordination, and strengthen arms and legs.

INSTRUCTIONS:

1. Sit with feet flat on the floor, knees, and ankles close together.

2. Swing arms out and above your head as legs move out to the sides.

3. Bring arms down as legs return to the starting position.

4. Do 10 repetitions.

57. **SINGLE-LEG CALF RAISES**

Single-leg calf raises strengthen calves and enhance flexibility, mobility, balance, and coordination.

INSTRUCTIONS:

1. Sit on a chair with feet flat on the ground.

2. Lift one leg straight out in front with the foot flexed.

3. Hold for 5 seconds.

4. Lower the foot and repeat 10 times on each leg.

58. **REACHING**

Reaching exercises improve coordination, balance, and stretch muscles.

INSTRUCTIONS:

1. Have a partner hold an object in front of you.

2. Extend your arms fully and reach for the object.

3. Repeat 20 times with your partner moving the object side-to-side and up-and-down.

59.   **SEATED OVERHEAD STRETCH**

The seated overhead stretch strengthens various upper body muscles and improves balance, posture, mobility, and flexibility.

INSTRUCTIONS:

1. Sit up straight in a chair with feet aligned shoulder-width apart.

2. Extend both arms fully over your head.

3. Lean to the right, feeling a gentle stretch on your left side.

4. Return to the starting position and repeat the stretch to the left side.

5. Perform 10 repetitions on each side, totaling 20 stretches.

60. **SEATED PEDALING**

Seated pedaling enhances balance, coordination, and strengthens leg muscles (quadriceps, calves, and hamstrings).

INSTRUCTIONS:

1. Sit on a chair with your back against the backrest, feet flat on the ground, aligned with your shoulders.

2. Lift your right foot and pedal it in a circular motion.

3. Repeat the circular motion with your left foot.

4. Alternate legs for at least 10 times.

LYING DOWN BALANCE EXERCISES

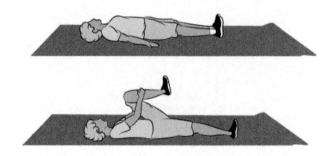

61.   FLOOR HAMSTRING STRETCHES

Floor hamstring stretches are great for strengthening the core, legs, arms, and hamstrings while improving hip stability, mobility, and flexibility to prevent falls.

INSTRUCTIONS:

1. Lie down flat on your yoga mat or the floor.

2. Bend your knees with your feet flat on the ground.

3. Lift both feet off the floor while keeping your knees bent.

4. Wrap your arms around your legs.

5. Hold this position for 15 seconds.

6. Repeat this process 3 times per leg for maximum benefits.

62.   4-POINT KNEELING

The 4-point kneeling exercise strengthens arms, legs, back, and abs while enhancing balance and coordination.

INSTRUCTIONS:

1. Kneel on the ground with palms shoulder-width apart, and toes curled under so heels are pointed up.

2. Lift your left knee off the ground and raise your left leg backward and upward.

3. Simultaneously, extend your right arm forward so that your left leg and right arm are aligned with your back. Hold for 5 seconds.

4. Repeat the process with the right leg and left arm.

5. Perform 10 repetitions on each leg.

63.   COMFORTABLE RECLINED TWIST

This exercise improves posture, strengthens muscles to prevent falls, massages hips and back, stretches and relaxes the spine, and lightly exercises abdominal muscles.

INSTRUCTIONS:

1. Lie down on a mat with your back pressed to the ground and knees bent.

2. Place your feet firmly on the floor, toes pointed forward.

3. Let your knees fall slowly to the floor on your right side while keeping both shoulders pressed to the floor. Feel the stretch in your left glute and lower back.

4. Bring your bent legs back to the starting position and drop the lower half of your body to your left side.

5. Repeat this process eight times on each side of your body.

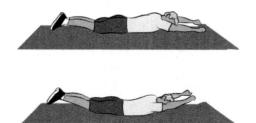

64. **SUPERMAN**

The Superman exercise targets multiple muscle groups, including the erector spinae muscles, back muscles, glutes, and muscles in the lower back. It improves posture, balance, and fall prevention.

INSTRUCTIONS:

1. Lie on your stomach on a mat with your legs extended and arms stretched forward.

2. Slowly lift your arms and legs about 5 inches off the floor until you feel a slight pressure in your lower back.

3. Contract your glutes and abs, and imagine lifting your belly button slightly off the ground as if you were flying (hence the name "Superman").

4. Hold this position for 2 seconds, maintaining regular breathing.

5. Return to the starting position.

6. Repeat this exercise 10 times.

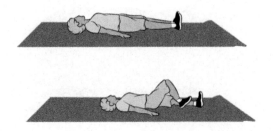

65. **HEEL SLIDES**

Heel slides are beneficial for building strength in the ankles, legs, and knees while increasing knee range of motion, making it helpful for knee injury or surgery recovery.

INSTRUCTIONS:

1. Lie down on your back on a mat or bed with your legs flat and straight.

2. Slide your right heel toward your glutes while bending your knee. If possible, grab your ankle with your hand and gently pull your heel back to increase the stretch.

3. Release your ankle and slide your heel back to the starting position, then slowly lay your leg flat on the bed or floor.

4. Repeat with your left heel.

5. Do 10 repetitions, alternating legs as you go.

WALKING BALANCE EXERCISES

66. **TIGHTROPE WALK**

The tightrope walk exercise focuses on balance and coordination while walking.

INSTRUCTIONS:

1. Stand up straight with your arms raised out to your sides and bow your head to look at your feet.

2. Walk slowly and deliberately forward in a straight line, placing your right leg in front of your left and then switching legs.

3. Walk as far as you can without falling over. Keep within arm's distance to a wall for support if needed.

4. You can also tape a line on the floor to help guide your walking path and maintain balance.

67.   GRAPEVINE

The grapevine exercise enhances balance and coordination, and you can use support if needed.

INSTRUCTIONS:

1. Stand with your feet hip-width apart, keeping your arms down at your sides.

2. Cross your right leg in front of your left one and step down.

3. Step out to the left with your left leg, returning to the hip-width apart position.

4. Cross your right leg behind your left leg.

5. Step out to the left again, returning to the hip-width apart position.

6. Repeat steps 3 and 4 to move across the room sideways.

7. Continue repeating the grapevine steps from one side of the room to the other.

68. **JOGGING IN PLACE**

Jogging in place improves balance, coordination, and overall fitness. Ensure you start at a comfortable pace.

INSTRUCTIONS:

1. Stand in place with your feet flat on the ground and your knees and ankles close together.

2. Lift your knees one at a time and pump your arms as if jogging.

3. Jog in place at your own pace, focusing on maintaining proper form and breathing.

4. You can use furniture for support if needed and take breaks when necessary.

5. Reach out to your doctor before starting this exercise to ensure it is safe for you.

69.   **HEEL-TOE WALKING**

Heel-toe walking strengthens the legs and ankles while improving balance.

INSTRUCTIONS:

1. Stand tall with your feet flat on the ground and your arms extended to the sides.

2. Keep your head up and your eyes focused straight ahead, using peripheral vision to see the floor and surroundings.

3. Place one foot in front of the other, ensuring you land on your heel first and then roll onto the balls of your feet and toes.

4. Walk deliberately with 20 steps for each leg.

70. **10,000 STEPS A DAY**

The 10,000 steps-a-day challenge encourages walking to improve overall physical and mental health.

INSTRUCTIONS:

1. Aim to walk 10,000 steps daily, which can be tracked using a pedometer or fitness tracker.

2. You can walk around your neighborhood, in nature, or even around your house while doing daily tasks.

3. Start slowly if needed, and gradually increase your steps over time.

4. Listen to your body, and consult your doctor if you have any concerns.

71. SIDESTEPPING

Sidestepping improves balance and heart health, but caution should be taken to avoid potential injuries.

INSTRUCTIONS:

1. Stand up straight with your feet together and slightly bend your knees.

2. Step to the right side with your right foot, then bring your left foot to touch your right foot.

3. Repeat this sideways stepping motion ten times per side, adjusting the pace for comfort.

4. Bend your knees deeper while side-stepping for increased intensity.

Variations:

- Banded side step: Attach a resistance band around your ankles to add resistance while sidestepping.

- Side shuffle with ground touches: Slide your foot along the floor to the side and tap your toes, alternating sides.

- Side step up: Step onto a low platform and push up to a standing position, alternating legs.

72. **MARCHING**

Marching is a low-impact exercise that improves leg strength, heart health, and blood circulation.

INSTRUCTIONS:

1. Stand up straight, near a wall if you need support.

2. Lift your left leg towards your chest, bending your knee, while keeping your back straight.

3. Slowly place your left leg back onto the ground and repeat the process with your right leg.

4. Continue alternating legs, performing 20 repetitions on each leg.

Tips: Focus on controlled movements and maintaining good balance. If you want to challenge yourself, perform the exercise at a slower pace to gain better control of your balance.

73.   WALKING ON HEELS AND TOES

Walking on heels and toes is an excellent warm-up exercise to improve balance, agility, and lower body strength.

INSTRUCTIONS:

1. Begin by walking normally back and forth across the room, ensuring you keep your back straight and gaze forward.

2. After a few regular steps, switch to walking on your toes for 15 seconds.

3. Next, walk on your heels for another 15 seconds.

4. Continue alternating between regular walking, walking on toes, and walking on heels.

STRENGTH TRAINING

Strength training exercises are one of the best things you can do for your overall health and well-being. They can help you lose weight, build muscle, improve your cardiovascular health, and reduce your risk of chronic diseases. But did you know that strength training can also help you age gracefully and live a longer, healthier life?

Let us examine some benefits of strength training exercises:

With an increase in age, our muscle mass naturally declines, which can lead to several problems, including weakness, fatigue, and an increased risk of falls. Strength training can help to slow down this muscle loss and keep our muscles strong and healthy.

Strong muscles are essential for maintaining good posture, balance, and coordination. They also help to protect our joints and reduce our risk of injuries. Strength training can also help to improve our metabolism and reduce our risk of obesity. Additional benefits of strength training exercises includes:

- Improved Memory
- Improved balance and coordination
- Reduced risk of chronic diseases such as heart disease, stroke, type 2 diabetes, and osteoporosis
- Improved mood and mental health
- Increased energy levels
- Better sleep quality
- Reduced stress levels
- Improved self-esteem

You can practice these strength training exercises using your body weight, or modify them with resistance bands and free weights. There are various strength training exercises that you can do in this book.

Strength training is one of the best things you can do for your overall health and well-being. It can help you age gracefully, live a longer, healthier life, and improve your memory, balance, and coordination.

LYING DOWN STRETCHES

74. **COBRA STRETCH**
Level: Easy

INSTRUCTIONS:

1. Lie face down on the floor with your legs extended behind you.

2. Place your hands on the floor beside your shoulders, fingers pointing forward.

3. Gently lift your upper body off the ground, using your hands for support.

4. Feel the stretch in your chest and back muscles.

5. Hold this position for 30 seconds, then rest for another 30 seconds.

6. Repeat the stretch three times.

75. **THREAD THE NEEDLE STRETCH**
Level: Easy/Medium

INSTRUCTIONS:

1. Begin on all fours, with hands shoulder-width apart and knees at 90 degrees.

2. Slide your right arm under your body toward the left side.

3. Keep moving your arm until your right shoulder touches the ground.

4. Your position should resemble the picture, with your palm facing up.

5. Hold this position for 20 seconds.

6. Switch sides and repeat the stretch.

7. Perform the exercise twice in total.

76. **CHILD'S POSE STRETCH**
Level: Medium

INSTRUCTIONS:

1. Start on your knees.

2. Lean your body back until your buttocks touch your heels.

3. While maintaining this contact, lower your torso to the floor and extend your arms forward.

4. Inhale and exhale normally while extending your arms as far as comfortable.

5. Hold this position for 30 seconds.

77. **WINDSHIELD WIPERS STRETCH**
Level: Hard

INSTRUCTIONS:

1. Lie on a mat with your knees bent and forming an angle, arms straight out to the sides.

2. Inhale deeply to prepare.

3. Exhale slowly as you lower both knees to the left side, emphasizing the stretch on the right side.

4. Focus on the stretch and exhale during the movement.

5. Hold this position for at least 5 seconds.

6. Repeat the exercise on the opposite side.

7. Perform this stretch on each side a total of 3 times.

78. **HAMSTRING STRETCH WITH RESISTANCE BAND**
Level: Medium

INSTRUCTIONS:

1. Lie on your back on a mat.

2. Loop the resistance band around your left foot, bending your knee to secure it. Hold the ends of the band with both hands.

3. Straighten your left leg and raise it toward the ceiling, using the band to adjust the stretch intensity.

4. Hold this position for 30 seconds.

5. Repeat the stretch on the opposite leg.

79. **TIGHT HAMSTRINGS STRETCH**
Level: Easy

INSTRUCTIONS:

1. Sit on a mat with your left leg extended in front of you.

2. Place the heel of your right foot on your left thigh.

3. Reach your arms towards the left leg and aim to grip the foot.

4. Gently pull the foot towards you to deepen the stretch.

5. Hold this position for 30 seconds.

6. Repeat the exercise for the other leg.

80. **RECLINED BUTTERFLY STRETCH**
Level: Medium

INSTRUCTIONS:

1. Sit on a mat.

2. Press the soles of your feet together, attempting to bring them close to your body.

3. While keeping your hands on your ankles, lie down again.

4. You can either gently push your feet towards your body or let your arms rest, allowing gravity to do the work.

5. Hold this position for 40 seconds.

SITTING STRETCHES

81. **TRICEP PULL**
Level: Easy

INSTRUCTIONS:

1. Raise your right arm above your head and bend it behind you.

2. Use your left hand to gently pull your right elbow towards your back.

3. Aim to touch your back as low as comfortable with your right hand for an enhanced stretch.

4. Hold this position for 20 seconds.

5. Repeat the stretch on the opposite side.

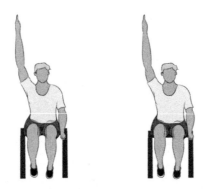

82. **LATISSIMUS STRETCH**
Level: Easy

INSTRUCTIONS:

1. Extend your right arm above your head and reach as far as possible.

2. Hold onto a chair with your left hand for support.

3. For a deeper stretch, imagine stretching your right shoulder toward the ceiling.

4. Maintain this stretch for 20 seconds.

5. Repeat the stretch on the opposite side.

83. **OVERHEAD STRETCH**
Level: Easy

INSTRUCTIONS:

1. Raise both arms above your head and interlace your fingers with palms facing up.

2. Stretch your arms upwards as much as comfortable.

3. For an enhanced stretch, visualize reaching your right shoulder toward the ceiling.

4. Hold this stretch for 20 seconds.

84. **SEATED FORWARD STRETCH**

Level: Easy

INSTRUCTIONS:

1. Raise both arms in front of you, keeping them straight.

2. Interlace your hands with palms facing you.

3. Extend your arms forward, allowing a slight curve in your upper back.

4. Feel the stretch in your upper back.

5. Hold this stretch for 30 seconds.

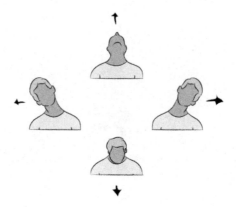

85. **NECK CIRCLES**
Level: Easy

INSTRUCTIONS:

1. Gently tilt your head to the left to feel a stretch on the right side. Hold for 5 seconds.

2. Repeat the stretch for the other three sides: right, up, and down.

3. Begin rotating your head in a clockwise direction to complete a full circle. The entire movement should take around 5 seconds.

4. Perform the circle motion 8 times.

86. **UPPER TRAP STRETCH**
Level: Easy

INSTRUCTIONS:

1. Sit upright on a chair.

2. Hold the right side of your head with your left hand.

3. Gently pull your head toward your left shoulder, feeling a mild stretch on the right side.

4. Hold the stretch for 30 seconds.

5. Repeat the stretch on the opposite side.

87. **LAT STRETCH**
Level: Easy

INSTRUCTIONS:

1. Sit up straight on a chair.

2. Hold the right side of the chair's seat with your right hand for stability.

3. Extend your left arm over your head.

4. Simultaneously lean your torso to the right side.

5. Hold this stretch for 10 seconds.

6. Repeat the stretch on the opposite side.

7. Perform this sequence 3 more times for each side.

88. **TORSO STRETCH**
Difficulty: Easy

INSTRUCTIONS:

1. Sit on a chair with your back straight and cross your legs.

2. Use your left hand to grasp the back of the chair and place your right hand on your left knee.

3. Rotate your torso towards the left by pushing your hands in the opposite direction.

4. Hold this stretch for 10 seconds.

5. Repeat the stretch on the other side.

89. **CALF RAISES**
Difficulty: Easy

INSTRUCTIONS:

1. Sit on a chair with your back straight.

2. Hold onto the sides of the chair's seat for stability.

3. Shift your weight onto the balls of your feet and raise your heels as high as you can.

4. You should feel a significant stretch in your calf muscles.

5. Hold the stretch for 5 seconds.

6. Repeat this movement 8 times.

90. **SEATED BACKBEND**

Difficulty: Easy

INSTRUCTIONS:

1. Sit on a chair with your back straight.

2. Place both hands around your lower back.

3. Press your hands down to create a gentle arch in your lower back.

4. Hold this position for about 10 seconds, focusing on controlled breathing.

5. Return to the starting position.

6. Perform this backbend stretch 5 times.

STANDING STRETCHES

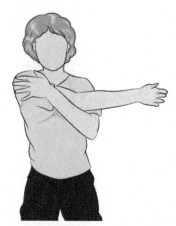

91. **CROSS-BODY SHOULDER STRETCH**
Difficulty: Easy

INSTRUCTIONS:

1. Stand with your feet shoulder-width apart.

2. Raise your right arm in front of you.

3. Use your left arm to grab your right elbow and gently pull it across your body towards your left shoulder (as shown).

4. Hold this stretch for approximately 20 seconds.

5. Repeat the stretch on the opposite side.

92. **CACTUS ARMS**
Difficulty: Easy

INSTRUCTIONS:

1. Stand with your feet shoulder-width apart and bend your arms to a 90° angle (like a cactus shape).

2. Gently stretch your arms backward as much as comfortable for 5 seconds.

3. Bring your arms in front of you with palms facing each other.

4. Push one arm against the other for 5 seconds.

5. Return to the starting position.

6. Repeat this exercise sequence 4 times.

93. **SHOULDER ROTATIONS**
Difficulty: Easy

INSTRUCTIONS:

1. Stand with your feet shoulder-width apart.

2. Begin by raising both shoulders towards your ears for 3 seconds.

3. Visualize moving your shoulders backward while retracting your shoulder blades for another 3 seconds.

4. Actively push your shoulders down for 3 seconds.

5. Complete the sequence by bringing your shoulders forward and slightly rounding your upper back, holding for 3 seconds.

6. Repeat the entire rotation cycle 2 more times.

94. **ABS EXTENSION**
Difficulty: Easy

INSTRUCTIONS:

1. Stand with your feet shoulder-width apart.

2. Gently engage your abdominal muscles and raise your arms towards the ceiling, creating a stretch in your abdomen.

3. Pull your shoulders back and push your pelvis forward, arching your lower back as shown.

4. Hold this stretch for approximately 15 seconds.

5. Return to the starting position.

6. Repeat this exercise sequence 3 times.

95. **LUNGE STRETCH**
Difficulty: Medium/Hard

INSTRUCTIONS:

1. Stand with your feet shoulder-width apart.

2. Engage your core as you lift your left leg off the floor.

3. Take a step forward into a lunge position, ensuring your left leg forms a 90° angle.

4. Place both hands on your left knee for stability.

5. Extend your right leg behind you as much as possible while keeping your left leg in the lunge position.

6. Hold this stretch for 20-30 seconds.

7. Repeat the stretch on the other side.

96. **STANDING QUAD STRETCH**
Difficulty: Medium

INSTRUCTIONS:

1. Stand with your feet shoulder-width apart.

2. Lift your left foot behind you and grasp it with your left hand.

3. Shift your body weight to your right leg.

4. Gently pull your foot towards your bottom until you feel a comfortable stretch in the quad. If you feel knee discomfort, stop the stretch.

5. Hold the stretch for around 30 seconds.

6. Repeat the stretch on the other leg.

97. **LEG SWINGS**
Difficulty: Medium

INSTRUCTIONS:

1. Place your hand against a wall or hold onto the back of a table or chair for balance.

2. Bend your right leg slightly and swing it forward as if you're kicking a ball, reaching the leg's highest point without compromising balance or torso alignment.

3. Swing the leg back behind you, not as far as the forward swing.

4. Perform 10-15 swings on one leg, then switch and repeat with the other leg.

98. **WAIST CIRCLES**
Difficulty: Easy

INSTRUCTIONS:

1. Stand with your feet shoulder-width apart, keeping your back straight and chin facing forward.

2. Place your hands on your waist.

3. Begin by slowly rotating your hips to the left (counterclockwise), as if you're drawing a large circle with your waist.

4. Complete 5 circles in the counterclockwise direction.

5. Repeat the movement by rotating your hips in a clockwise direction for 5 more circles.

99.   QUAD STRETCH
Difficulty: Easy

INSTRUCTIONS:

1. Stand with your feet shoulder-width apart.

2. Lift your left foot behind you and hold onto it with your left hand, shifting your body weight onto your right leg.

3. Gently pull your foot towards your bottom to feel a stretch in the front of your thigh (quad). Stop if you feel any discomfort in your knee.

4. Hold the stretch for about 30 seconds.

5. Repeat the stretch on the other leg.

100. **HIP ROLLOVER**
Difficulty: Hard

INSTRUCTIONS:

1. Lie on a mat with your knees bent, feet flat on the floor, and arms extended straight to the sides.

2. Inhale deeply. As you exhale, slowly drop both knees to the left side, focusing on stretching the muscles on the right side of your body.

3. Exhale slowly and maintain the stretch for at least 5 seconds.

4. Return your knees to the starting position.

5. Repeat the exercise by dropping your knees to the right side, focusing on the left-side stretch.

6. Perform this exercise a total of 3 times on each side.

CONCLUSION

I want to congratulate you for not just purchasing this book but for also taking the time to read it up to this length. I believe you enjoyed the exercises in this book and found them easy to do.

Now that you are done performing all the exercises explained and illustrated in this book, go out there and continue to live the healthy life you have always wanted. Go forth and do the things that used to seem impossible because rest assured you are now stronger, more balanced, and have higher resistance.

Before you reach the last page, kindly take your time to study the content on the bonus page, where you will get anti-aging supplements, food, and memory training book recommendations.

Live well, and enjoy your life forever young!

BONUS PAGE

EXERCISE RULES TO LONGEVITY

- Exercise at least 3 times a week
- Develop a daily walking habit – preferably in the morning

GOOD EATING HABITS

- Eat less often (1-2 times daily)
- Practice autophagy through intermittent fasting (not eating for 16 hours)
- Always stay hydrated
- Eat sweet potatoes instead of other starchy foods like cold cereal, rice, and bread.

FOODS TO EAT FOR LONGEVITY

- Colored Vegetables (Polyphenols): Red Onions.
- Cruciferous Vegetables: Broccoli, Cauliflower.
- Leafy Greens, Kale.
- Plums.
- Berries: Raspberries, Blueberries.
- Animal and Fish Fats, Eggs (at least two eggs daily), Coconut Oil, Olive Oil, Avocado Oil.

FOODS TO AVOID FOR LONGEVITY

- Sugar
- Carbohydrates
- Bread
- Dairy
- Sugar-Sweetened Beverages
- Packaged Candies and Cookies
- Salty Snacks: Potato Chips, Plantain Chips.
- Processed Meats: Sausage, Hot Dogs, Bacon.

ANTI-AGING SUPPLEMENTS FOR STRONG IMMUNITY

IN THE MORNING AFTER BREAKFAST
- Vitamin D3 + K2 – Vitamin D3 5000IU with K2100-200Mcg
- Quercetin 500 mg, Zinc 25 mg, Bromelain
- Vitamin B1 (Thiamin)
- Turmeric Curcumin 2250 mg

FOR BRAIN IMPROVEMENT
- MCT Oil (cook or put in salad)
- Coconut Oil – 1tbspoon in the morning
- Avocado and Olive Oil (to cook)

IN THE EVENING AFTER DINNER
- Melatonin 10 mg
- Omega3 1500 mg
- Magnesium 1000mg

MEMORY IMPROVEMENT BOOKS FOR ADULTS:
- Memory Games for Seniors & Adults
- Extra Large Word Search for Seniors
- Memory Activity Book for Seniors
- Memory Activity Book & Easy Puzzles for Seniors

DIET IMPROVEMENT BOOK:
- Anti-Inflammatory & Alkaline Diet

THANK YOU

Thanks for your purchase.

We hope you found this book really helpful in making you feel healthier and look younger as you observed the simple and functional exercises therein.

Kindly leave your feedback on this book on the product page as it will help spread the good news about it and inspire us to do more.

Thanks once again for your purchase.

Printed in Great Britain
by Amazon

39661998R10066